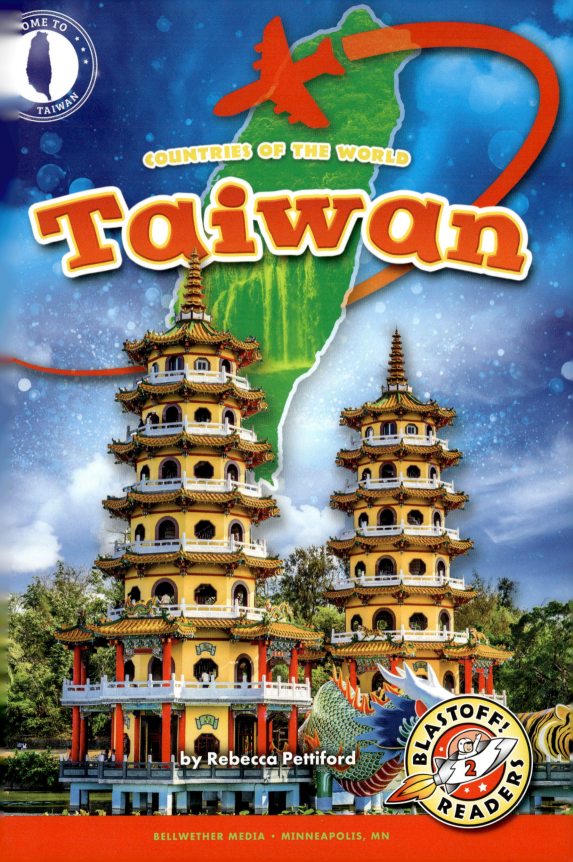

Blastoff! Readers are carefully developed by literacy experts to build reading stamina and move students toward fluency by combining standards-based content with developmentally appropriate text.

LEVELS

 Level 1 provides the most support through repetition of high-frequency words, light text, predictable sentence patterns, and strong visual support.

 Level 2 offers early readers a bit more challenge through varied sentences, increased text load, and text-supportive special features.

 Level 3 advances early-fluent readers toward fluency through increased text load, less reliance on photos, advancing concepts, longer sentences, and more complex special features.

★ **Blastoff! Universe**

Reading Level

This edition first published in 2026 by Bellwether Media, Inc.

No part of this publication may be reproduced in whole or in part without written permission of the publisher. For information regarding permission, write to Bellwether Media, Inc., Attention: Permissions Department, 3500 American Blvd W, Suite 150, Bloomington, MN 55431.

Library of Congress Cataloging-in-Publication Data

LC record for Taiwan available at: https://lccn.loc.gov/2025015124

Text copyright © 2026 by Bellwether Media, Inc. BLASTOFF! READERS and associated logos are trademarks and/or registered trademarks of Bellwether Media, Inc. Bellwether Media is a division of FlutterBee Education Group.

Editor: Betsy Rathburn   Designer: Laura Sowers

Printed in the United States of America, North Mankato, MN.

Table of Contents

All About Taiwan 4
Land and Animals 6
Life in Taiwan 12
Taiwan Facts 20
Glossary 22
To Learn More 23
Index 24

All About Taiwan

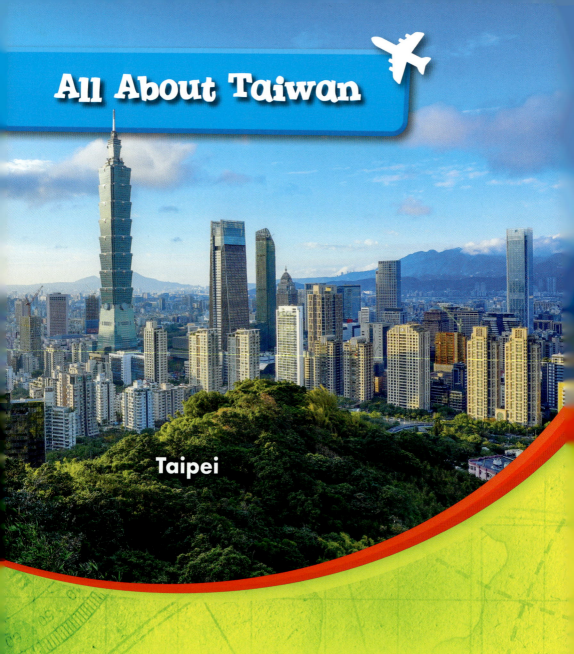

Taipei

Taiwan is a small island country in East Asia. Taipei is the capital city.

Taiwan is known for its night markets and delicious street food.

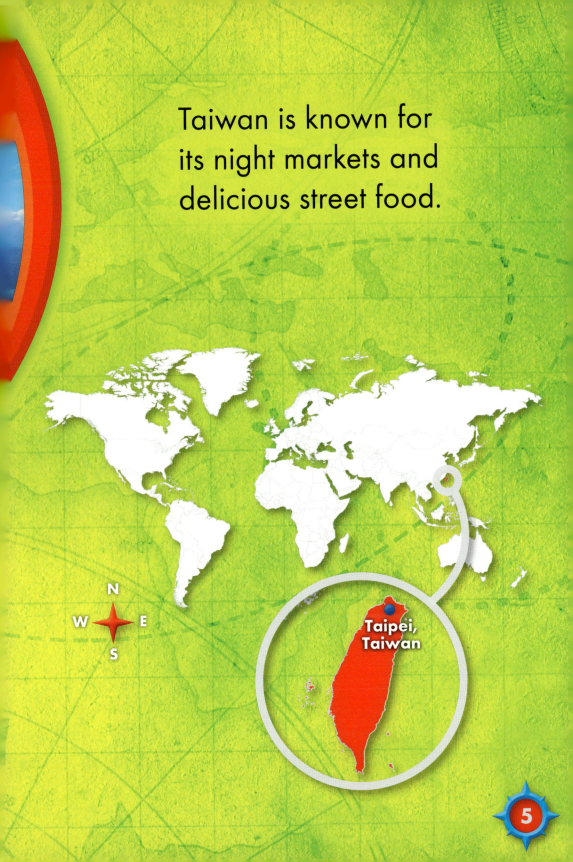

Land and Animals

Mountains and hills cover much of Taiwan. **Evergreen** forests grow in the mountains.

Short rivers run through mountain **gorges**. Palm trees and **bamboo** grow in the **lowlands**.

bamboo forest

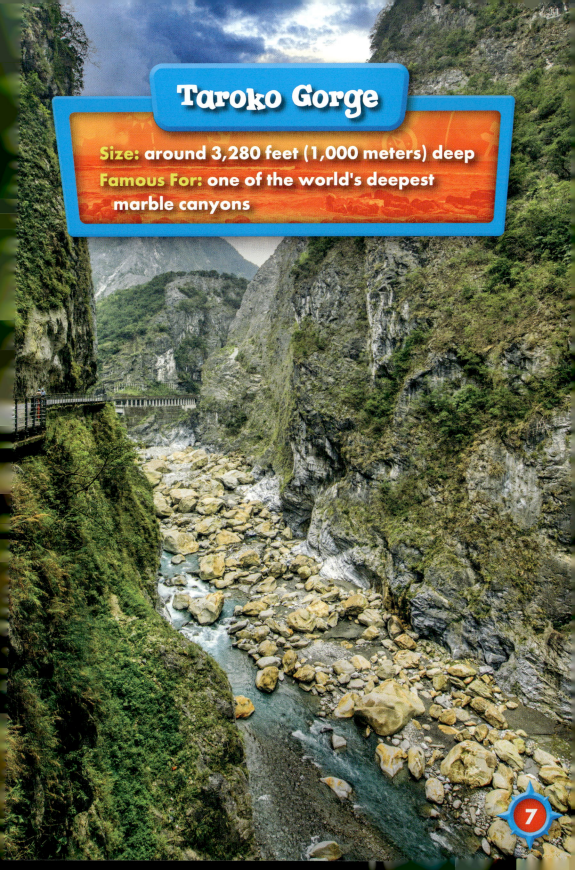

Taroko Gorge

Size: around 3,280 feet (1,000 meters) deep

Famous For: one of the world's deepest marble canyons

Taiwan is warm and **humid**. Rain is heaviest in the east and in the mountains.

Typhoons strike the island in the summer.

typhoon

Flying foxes search for fruit. Bears hunt in forests. Snakes slide through rocky hills.

Taiwan blue magpie

Animals of Taiwan

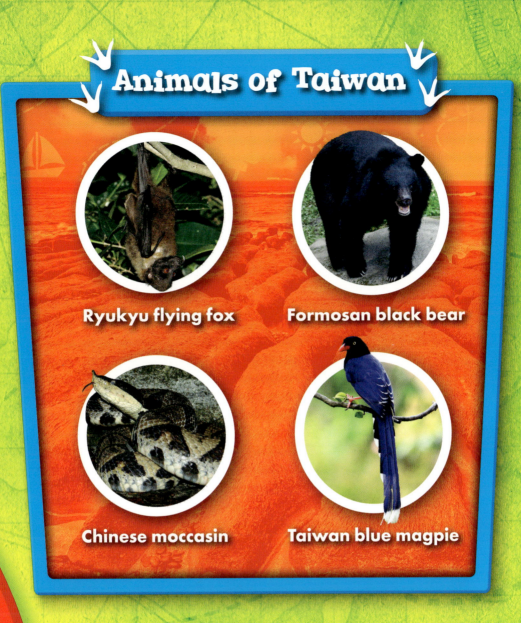

Ryukyu flying fox

Formosan black bear

Chinese moccasin

Taiwan blue magpie

Taiwan blue magpies fly high. They are a **symbol** of Taiwan.

Life in Taiwan

Most people in Taiwan have **ancestors** from China. Mandarin is the main language.

Many people live in cities. Most people practice **Buddhism** or **Taoism**.

Buddhist temple

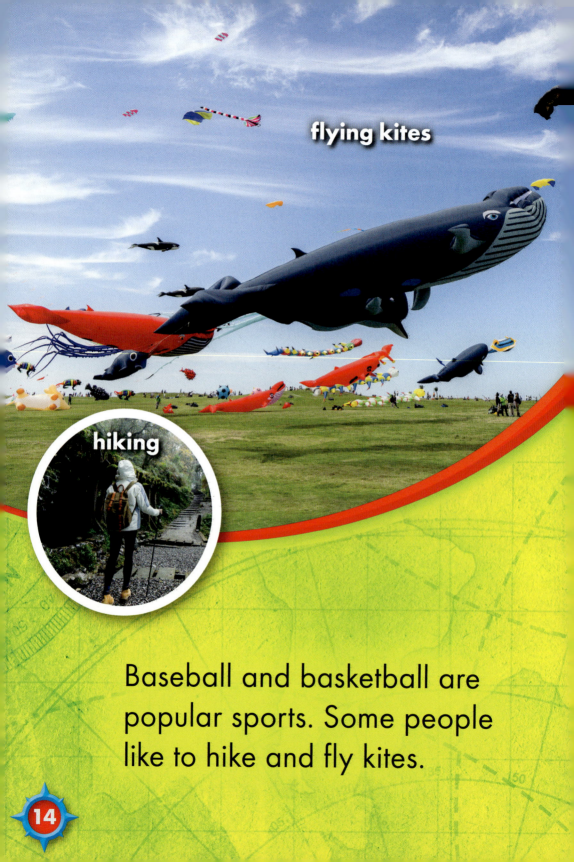

flying kites

hiking

Baseball and basketball are popular sports. Some people like to hike and fly kites.

Night markets are open late. People enjoy street food and live music!

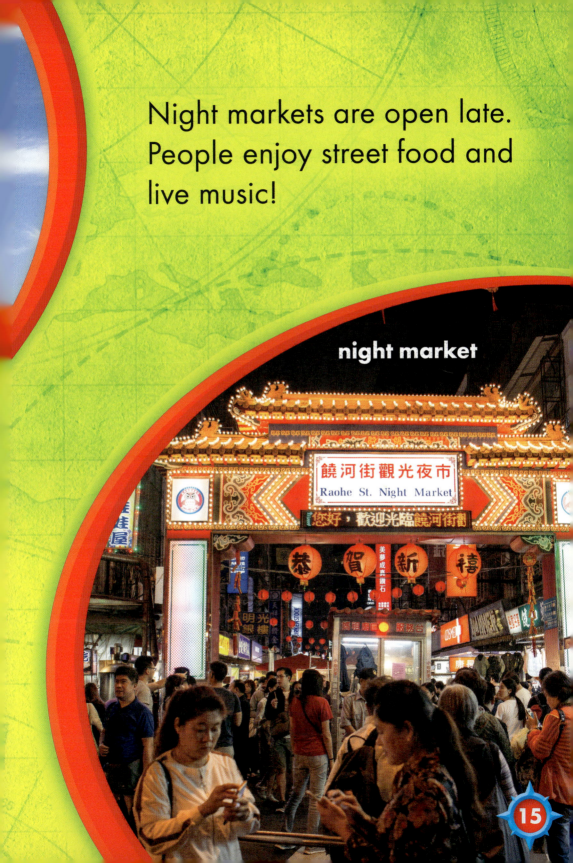

night market

Shaved ice comes in many fruit flavors. Many people drink sweet bubble tea.

Taiwanese Foods

shaved ice

bubble tea

beef noodle soup

stinky tofu

bubble tea

Beef noodle soup is a popular dish. Stinky tofu has many fans!

Dragon Boat Festival

People watch fireworks for Taiwanese New Year each winter. People race boats during the Dragon Boat **Festival**.

Taiwanese people **celebrate** all year long!

Taiwan Facts

Size:
13,892 square miles
(35,980 square kilometers)

Population:
23,595,274 (2024)

National Holiday:
National Day (October 10)

Main Language:
Mandarin

Capital City:
Taipei

Famous Face

Name: Rainie Yang

Famous For: singer and actress

Religions

folk religion: 10%

Buddhist: 35%

other: 22%

Taoist: 33%

Top Landmarks

Dragon and Tiger Pagodas

Queen's Head rock

Taipei 101

Glossary

ancestors—relatives who lived long ago

bamboo—a tall, tree-like grass that grows in warm regions

Buddhism—a religion of eastern and central Asia based on the teachings of Buddha, the founder of Buddhism

celebrate—to do something special or fun for an event, occasion, or holiday

evergreen—related to trees and plants that stay green all year

festival—a time or event of celebration

gorges—narrow valleys between hills or mountains

humid—having a lot of water in the air

lowlands—lands that are fairly flat and not high above sea level

symbol—an object that stands for an idea or a belief

Taoism—a religion from east Asia that centers around living in harmony with the natural world

typhoons—huge, powerful, and harmful storms that often happen in Southeast Asia

To Learn More

AT THE LIBRARY

Chang, Kirsten. *Mandarin*. Minneapolis, Minn.: Bellwether Media, 2026.

Davies, Monika. *China*. Minneapolis, Minn.: Bellwether Media, 2023.

Pettiford, Rebecca. *Malaysia*. Minneapolis, Minn.: Bellwether Media, 2026.

ON THE WEB

FACTSURFER

Factsurfer.com gives you a safe, fun way to find more information.

1. Go to www.factsurfer.com.

2. Enter "Taiwan" into the search box and click 🔍.

3. Select your book cover to see a list of related content.

Index

animals, 10, 11
baseball, 14
basketball, 14
Buddhism, 12
capital (see Taipei)
cities, 12
Dragon Boat Festival, 18
East Asia, 4
food, 5, 15, 16, 17
forests, 6, 10
gorges, 6, 7
hike, 14
hills, 6, 10
island, 4, 9
kites, 14
lowlands, 6
Mandarin, 12, 13
map, 5
mountains, 6, 8
music, 15
night markets, 5, 15
people, 12, 14, 15, 16, 18, 19

rain, 8
rivers, 6
say hello, 13
summer, 9
Taipei, 4, 5
Taiwan facts, 20–21
Taiwanese New Year, 18
Taoism, 12
Taroko Gorge, 7
typhoons, 9
winter, 18

The images in this book are reproduced through the courtesy of: Sean Pavone, front cover, p. 21 (Dragon and Tiger Pagodas); LiaSte, p. 3; Feng Cheng, pp. 4-5; Kit Leong, p. 6; Alberto, pp. 6-7; leochen66, pp. 8-9; Minase, p. 9; muhammadadeel007, pp. 10-11; photoncatcher, p. 11 (Formosan black bear); Hank Asia, p. 11 (Chinese moccasin); Agami Photo Agency, p. 11 (Ryukyu flying fox); WU CHIH-SHENG, p. 11 (Taiwan blue magpie); Sanga Park, p. 12; Horizon International Images/ Alamy Stock Photo, pp. 12-13; leungchopan, p. 14 (hiking); leungchopan, pp. 14-15; kuponjabah, p. 15; John, p. 16 (shaved ice); ROHE Creative Studio, p. 16 (bubble tea); aaron choi, p. 16 (beef noodle soup); CarlosTamsui, p. 16 (stinky tofu); PhaiApirom, p. 17; asiapics/ Alamy Stock Photo, pp. 18-19; Osman Bugra Nuvasil, p. 20 (flag); VCG/ Getty Images, p. 20 (Rainie Yang); Sean Hsu, p. 21 (Queen's Head rock); bennnn, p. 21 (Taipei 101); catmanc, p. 23.